Openness

Published in the United States of America by Cherry Lake Publishing
Ann Arbor, Michigan
www.cherrylakepublishing.com

Reading Adviser: Marla Conn, MS, Ed., Literacy specialist, Read-Ability, Inc.
Book Designer: Jennifer Wahi
Illustrator: Jeff Bane

Photo Credits: ©TY Lim/Shutterstock, 5; ©Daniel Jedzura/Shutterstock, 7; ©szefei/Shutterstock, 9; ©MR. AEKALAK CHIAMCHAROEN/Shutterstock, 11; ©George Rudy/Shutterstock, 13; ©Sharomka/Shutterstock, 15, 23; ©Syda Productions/Shutterstock, 17; ©Sunny studio/Shutterstock, 19; ©fizkes/Shutterstock, 21; Cover, 6, 10, 12, Jeff Bane; Various vector images throughout courtesy of Shutterstock.com

Library of Congress Cataloging-in-Publication Data has been filed and is available at catalog.loc.gov

Printed in the United States of America
Corporate Graphics

About the author: Katie Marsico is the author of more than 200 reference books for children and young adults. She lives with her husband and six children near Chicago, Illinois.

About the illustrator: Jeff Bane and his two business partners own a studio along the American River in Folsom, California, home of the 1849 Gold Rush. When Jeff's not sketching or illustrating for clients, he's either swimming or kayaking in the river to relax.

Not all feelings are fun.

Sometimes we **ignore** them.

We also ignore the problems that cause them.

Think about the last time you cried.

Did you feel **relieved**?

Openness does that!

Being open to feelings is healthy.

It's how we deal with them.

Feelings such as sadness aren't bad.

Not being **mindful** of them is.

How do you feel right now?

When we're not open, we get stuck.

We **focus** on the past.

We miss out on new experiences.

What is something new you'd like to try?

Fighting feelings leads to **stress**.

It makes us moody and tired.

Sometimes it even makes us sick.

Crying doesn't always feel good.

Yet tears show our openness.

They prove we feel things.

Talking is important too.

It often helps us sort out our feelings.

It also makes other people aware of them.

Openness clears our mind.

Take a breath.

We need a clear mind to be mindful.

Many people do activities to become more mindful.

Some do **yoga** or **meditate**.

Others keep a journal.

Openness changes how we see the world.

We still face problems.

Yet we're open to using feelings to solve them!

How can you be mindful today?

glossary

focus (FOH-kuhs) to give your attention to

ignore (ig-NOR) to pay no attention to something

meditate (MED-ih-tate) to train your mind to relax and focus

mindful (MINDE-ful) aware of your body, mind, and feelings

openness (OH-puhn-nehs) the act of allowing yourself to experience and deal with feelings

relieved (rih-LEEVD) no longer feeling upset

stress (STRES) worry that weighs heavily on your mind

yoga (YOH-guh) poses, breathing, and sometimes meditation and chanting that provide balance and good health

index